God the Father's Love

God the Father's Love

A Journey Through Scripture for Catholic Families

Colleen Pressprich • Illustrated by Amy Heyse

OSV
Our Sunday Visitor
Huntington, Indiana

Nihil Obstat
Msgr. Michael Heintz, Ph.D.
Censor Librorum

Imprimatur
✠ Kevin C. Rhoades
Bishop of Fort Wayne-South Bend
September 26, 2023

The *Nihil Obstat* and *Imprimatur* are official declarations that a book is free from doctrinal or moral error. It is not implied that those who have granted the *Nihil Obstat* and *Imprimatur* agree with the contents, opinions, or statements expressed.

29 28 27 26 25 24 1 2 3 4 5 6 7 8 9

Our Sunday Visitor Publishing Division
Our Sunday Visitor, Inc.
200 Noll Plaza
Huntington, IN 46750
www.osv.com
1-800-348-2440

ISBN: 978-1-68192-998-9 (Inventory No. T2733)
1. RELIGION—Christian Living—Family & Relationships.
2. RELIGION—Christian Living—Inspirational.
3. RELIGION—Christianity—Catholic.
eISBN: 978-1-68192-999-6
LCCN: 2023949014

Cover design: Tyler Ottinger
Interior design: Amanda Falk
Cover and interior art: Amy Heyse

PRINTED IN THE UNITED STATES OF AMERICA

For Mary, Mia, Rosalind, and Thomas, may you always know the depth of the Father's love for you. (C. P.)

To Kevin, Holly, and Mayumi. I love you very much. Kevin, thank you for embodying the love of our heavenly Father to our girls. (A. H.)

CONTENTS

Introduction for Parents 8

Introduction for Children 11

Deuteronomy 1:30–31 — The Father Will Fight for You 13

Jeremiah 1:5 — The Father's Love Is Intentional 15

Isaiah 54:10 — The Father's Love Is Enduring 17

Jeremiah 29:11–14 — The Father Has Plans for You 19

Isaiah 41:13 — The Father's Love Means You Don't Have to Fear 21

Luke 12:22–27 — The Father Is Dependable 23

Luke 11:11–13 — The Father Wants to Give You Good Things 25

John 3:16 — The Father's Love Is Sacrificial 27

Proverbs 3:12 — The Father Loves Us Enough to Discipline Us 29

Isaiah 64:7 — God the Father Forms Us Gently 31

Matthew 6:6 — The Father Sees What Is Done in Secret 33
Luke 12:6–7 — The Father Notices Every Single Thing about You 35
Genesis 1:27 — The Father Made Us to Be Like Him 37
John 14:1–2 — God the Father Has a Place for You 39
James 1:17 — God Is the Father of Lights 41
Matthew 22:37–38 — God Wants to Be the One You Love the Most 43
1 John 3:1–2 — The Father Calls You His Child 45
Psalm 33:11 — God's Plans Stand Forever 47
Romans 8:31–32 — God Is on Your Side 49
Isaiah 49:15 — God Won't Forget You 51
Going Further 52
Notes for Parents 53

Introduction for Parents

The LORD called to Samuel, who answered, "Here I am." He ran to Eli and said, "Here I am. You called me." "I did not call you," Eli answered. "Go back to sleep." So he went back to sleep. Again the LORD called Samuel, who rose and went to Eli. "Here I am," he said. "You called me." But he answered, "I did not call you, my son. Go back to sleep." Samuel did not yet recognize the LORD, since the word of the LORD had not yet been revealed to him. The LORD called Samuel again, for the third time. Getting up and going to Eli, he said, "Here I am. You called me." Then Eli understood that the LORD was calling the youth. So he said to Samuel, "Go to sleep, and if you are called, reply, 'Speak, LORD, for your servant is listening.'" When Samuel went to sleep in his place, the LORD came and stood there, calling out as before: Samuel, Samuel! Samuel answered, "Speak, for your servant is listening." (1 Samuel 3:4–10)

I have always loved this story from Scripture, but it took on new meaning when I became a mother. Young Samuel hears a voice and runs to Eli, because Eli is the person with whom he has a relationship. He expects Eli to be calling him, for though they are not biological father and son, Samuel has been left in Eli's care. And Eli does not get angry at the boy for waking him up; he just tells him, as any parent would, to go back to sleep.

The Bible tells us, "Samuel did not yet recognize the Lord." God is the one speaking, but Samuel can't recognize God's voice; he doesn't know what God sounds like. Eli, who does know God, discerns that it is the Lord who called the boy, and Eli teaches him how to respond.

This relationship between Samuel and Eli — the trust and receptivity Samuel feels toward the man who is a father figure in his life — makes it possible for Samuel to enter into a relationship with God. And what a fruitful relationship it is!

That's at the heart of our jobs as parents: to teach our children to recognize God's call and to guide them in the way of their response. For God will surely call each of our children, just as He calls each of us.

So how do we cut through the noise of the world to help our kids hear the still, small voice of God?

The answer to that question is found in the pages of the Bible, God's living and breathing word. Introducing our children to Scripture will help prepare them to encounter God in their lives and to recognize the sound of His voice.

A wrong understanding of who God is can damage our hearts and make us incapable of accepting the love He offers. So many of us have been hurt in our lives by fathers or father figures who have not loved us well, or perhaps we have struggled to see and understand the way God has worked in our lives. If that's you, please know that you aren't alone. There is hope and support for your relationship with God the Father.

Luckily, the Father Heart of God is laid bare in the pages of the Bible. In Scripture, we encounter His love, His longing, His passionate care for each individual He has created. Your child is known and loved by the Father, just as deeply as you are, and in this book, I aim to help you and your child(ren) to discover that truth. Together, we will dive into twenty different passages of Scripture that reveal God the Father's love for us. I'll guide you through the process of reading and relating to Scripture as a family. At the end of each chapter, I've included conversation starters to help guide your reading and discussion. Additionally, the "Notes for Parents" section at the end of the book is designed to provide you with additional food for thought and possible conversation.

In the pages of this book, I hope you will encounter the Father Heart of God for yourself — perhaps for the first time — and find the words and confidence to guide your children along the first steps of their journey with God.

FINDING THE RIGHT PASSAGES

Helping my children develop a deep and lasting relationship with God is my highest priority. Like many Catholic families, we have multiple children's Bibles in our home. Our kids are familiar with the stories of Adam and Eve, Moses, Noah, and many others. The narratives are the easiest pieces of the Bible to share with kids, because they are stories. Children's Bibles typically leave out sections of Scripture that are not structured as narratives or deemed too difficult for children to understand. Although children might not be ready to encounter the entirety of the prophets or the intricacies of Leviticus, there are many lesser-known passages that show us who God is by revealing His heart — the heart of our loving Father.

St. Gregory the Great wrote that we ought to "learn the heart of God in the words of God so that [we] long more ardently for eternity." That is the goal of this book: to help you and your children learn God's heart. Throughout this book, we will look at who God is, what He does, and how He loves us.

The passages included in this book were carefully chosen to speak to the hearts of children. They each contain a truth about God's identity as a loving Father and their identity as His beloved children. Alongside each Scripture passage is a short reflection, followed by a few conversation starters and a prayer response. The conversation starters are meant to help spark discussions about faith with your children and to help you gain greater insight into what they're thinking and feeling. This information is invaluable as you guide them into a relationship with God. The goal of the discussion questions is to help children understand that God is speaking through His word, even today. These questions provide a framework to guide you as you help your children understand what He's saying.

MEMORIZATION OF VERSES

In my early twenties, I was a missionary with Life Teen. We lived in community — serving, praying, and following a rule of life modeled after the Rule of Saint Benedict. We prayed the Liturgy of the Hours three times a day. If you've never come across this beautiful prayer of the Church before, I would encourage you to look it up. It's a set of prayers based on Scripture that priests, religious, and lay people throughout the world use. It is mostly psalms, though other Bible passages are included as well. Because the prayers repeat in four-week cycles, by the end of my year, I knew most of the psalms and prayers by heart. To this day, these are the first words that spring to mind when I am in doubt, trouble, or sorrow — even when I'm in the midst of great joy. Now, as a parent, I try to pray the Liturgy of the Hours out loud with my children. I want them to hear the verses just as I did and to slowly absorb God's word until they know it by heart.

There is incredible value in memorizing Scripture passages. Memorization, combined with discussion and reflection, can make all the difference in your child's relationship with God. This combination can help children internalize many truths about themselves and the world: that they are loved; that they are valued for who they are, not what they do; that God is dependable; that His word is enduring, even through storms. As Scripture becomes part of their lives, they learn to know and recognize God's voice. And when God's voice is the first they hear in their head, no matter the situation — well, that is very powerful indeed.

Introduction for Children

The Bible is a love story. When we read it, we learn about who God is and how He loves us. Because the Bible is God's word, it is unlike any other book we will ever read. It is alive! This means that even though it was written a long time ago, God still speaks to us through it.

Did you know that when the words of the Bible were written down, God knew that someday, thousands of years down the road, you would read them? When He inspired the writers, He had you in mind! Isn't that incredible?

God loves you so much that He wants to talk to you. When we read the Bible, we are listening to God's voice. Let's find out what He wants to tell us about who He is.

THE TRINITY

As Catholics, we believe in the Trinity: God is three Persons in one God. Think about a clover. Have you ever plucked one from the ground? Each clover is one plant, but it has three leaves. Clover gives us a sense of God's nature. He is one God, but He is also three Persons: the Father, the Son, and the Holy Spirit. Each of these Persons is distinct. It's important that we get to know each of Them!

In this book, we are going to get to know God the Father better by reading His words from the Bible and talking about what they mean. Every passage we will read is God's voice speaking to you. God chose these words just for you. Isn't that amazing?

God cannot lie. He is Truth itself, so He simply never would say or do anything untrue. It would go against who He is. That means that when we read Scripture, which is His word, we can trust it.

As we read these Bible passages, let's pay attention to what God is saying to us about who He is and what He promises to each of us.

The Father Will Fight for You

The LORD, your God, who goes before you, is the one who will fight for you, just as he acted with you before your very eyes in Egypt, as well as in the wilderness, where you saw how the LORD, your God, carried you, as one carries his own child, all along your journey until you arrived at this place. (Deuteronomy 1:30–31)

There will be times in your life when it is going to be easy to know that God is close to you. Sometimes God is going to move in big ways in your life, like when He sent the plagues to Egypt or parted the Red Sea to free His people.

There are also going to be times in your life when it will be harder to see what God is doing. Sometimes He moves in small ways. Other times, His ways seem hidden altogether.

This is why the Israelites had a hard time in the wilderness. God wasn't doing big things anymore, so they thought He had forgotten them. But He hadn't. He was still with them, still helping them, and still loving them. He provided for them and kept them safe in the desert for forty years.

He will do the same for you. In the big moments and the small ones, God will be by your side to carry you and fight for you, no matter what.

Conversation Starters

- Have you ever experienced a time when you knew that God was fighting for you?
- How does it make you feel to think about God the Father carrying you? Fighting for you?

Prayer

Dear Father, thank You for being with me in every moment of my life. Thank You for the big and small ways that You are helping me right now. Help me to trust that You are here, even if I can't see You. Amen.

The Father's Love Is Intentional

Before I formed you in the womb I knew you. (Jeremiah 1:5)

God spoke these words to Jeremiah, one of the prophets in the Old Testament. Because God's word is alive, we also know that He meant them for us, too.

Even before you were born, God knew you. He saw you. He had a plan for you. He knew what color of hair you would have and how tall you would be. He knew what your giggles would sound like and how your voice would change when you get mad. He knew what your favorite foods would be and which ones you would hate.

What an amazing thing that is! God knew you before you even existed, and He loved you already.

Conversation Starters

- What do you feel when you think about the fact that God knew you before you were growing inside your mother's womb?
- What is your favorite thing about yourself? Why do you think God chose to create you that way?

Prayer

Dear God, please help me to remember that You know all of me and love me. Amen.

The Father's Love Is Enduring

Though the mountains fall away
and the hills be shaken,
my love shall never fall away from you
nor my covenant of peace be shaken,
says the LORD, who has mercy on you. (Isaiah 54:10)

During an earthquake, the plates of the earth's crust grind together. When that happens, the ground shakes — sometimes so violently that mountains do fall down. If you've ever been in an earthquake, you know how scary it can be. If you haven't experienced one, can you imagine how it would feel to be going about your day and suddenly the walls of your house start to shake?

In this passage from the Book of Isaiah, God tells us that sometimes the things we believe are immovable, like mountains and hills, actually do move. But His love never changes.

God's love for you is unconditional. No matter what you do, there will never be a moment when God does not love you and does not want to be with you. There will never be a moment when He loves you any less than He already does. Think about a time you were your grouchiest, grumpiest self. God loved you even then!

Conversation Starters

- What is something that you can always count on?
- Is it hard to love someone when they are grouchy?
- Do you think God ever has trouble loving someone? Why or why not?

Prayer

Dear Father, thank You for always loving me, no matter what we do or how we behave. Thank You for never leaving us, even in the scariest moments of our lives. Amen.

The Father Has Plans for You

For I know well the plans I have in mind for you — oracle of the LORD — plans for your welfare and not for woe, so as to give you a future of hope. When you call me, and come and pray to me, I will listen to you. When you look for me, you will find me. Yes, when you seek me with all your heart, I will let you find me — oracle of the LORD — and I will change your lot; I will gather you together from all the nations and all the places to which I have banished you — oracle of the LORD — and bring you back to the place from which I have exiled you. (Jeremiah 29:11–14)

God has a great adventure planned for you. Did you know that?

Would you like to go on this adventure with Him? Only you can choose. Only you can say yes when God asks. No one can make that decision for you, not even God Himself, because God gave you free will. In order to discover what God has planned for you, you have to go looking for Him and ask.

God has plans for you. Big plans. Beautiful plans. Plans beyond your wildest dreams.

Are you ready to find out what they are? As you learn to listen to and follow God's voice, His plans will unfold before you like a beautiful flower.

Conversation Starters

- What kind of adventure do you think God has in store for you? What do you want it to be?
- God has exciting plans for you! What does that tell you about who He is?

Prayer

Dear God, thank You for what You have planned for my life. I want to join the adventure You have in mind for me. Amen.

The Father's Love Means You Don't Have to Fear

For I am the LORD, your God,
who grasp your right hand;
It is I who say to you, Do not fear,
I will help you. (Isaiah 41:13)

Sometimes the world can be scary. There are natural disasters, diseases, poor people, and crimes. Our world is a big world with big problems. Bad things sometimes happen to us and the people we love.

God doesn't say that the world isn't scary. He knows it can be. But we don't have to be afraid, because He is with us. He never leaves our side.

In the Bible, God tells His people over and over again that they shouldn't be afraid. When they were stuck in the desert without food or water … when ferocious armies chased them … when they weren't sure that they could remain faithful to His commandments … He always said the same thing: "Don't be scared; I'm here to help."

Conversation Starters

- Is there anything you are afraid of? Have you ever told God about it or asked for His help?
- What is God the Father's promise to us in this passage?

PRAYER

Dear Lord, please remind me that You are with me when I am afraid or when things happen that I am not expecting. Thank You for never leaving me alone. Amen.

The Father Is Dependable

He said to [his] disciples, "Therefore I tell you, do not worry about your life and what you will eat, or about your body and what you will wear. For life is more than food and the body more than clothing. Notice the ravens: they do not sow or reap; they have neither storehouse nor barn, yet God feeds them. How much more important are you than birds! Can any of you by worrying add a moment to your life-span? If even the smallest things are beyond your control, why are you anxious about the rest? Notice how the flowers grow. They do not toil or spin. But I tell you, not even Solomon in all his splendor was dressed like one of them." (Luke 12:22–27)

The world around us is full of wondrous things! Have you ever noticed a butterfly's wings or the translucence of a praying mantis? What about the color of the sunrise or the way water sparkles when light hits it?

God created all of those things — and not just randomly. He planned each and every part of them, down to the teeniest, tiniest detail, yet none of them matches the miracle that you are.

You were created in God's image and likeness. You are His most precious creation. You can be sure that if He makes it possible for the smallest blades of grass to grow, He will take care of you.

Conversation Starters

- What's your favorite part of God's creation? Why?
- Have you ever thought about what God felt when He was making the animals and flowers and trees? What do you think it was like?

Prayer

Dear Lord, thank You for the wonder of creation. Thank You for Your imagination and creativity in all that You have designed. Please help us to never stop admiring what You have made and to remember that You love us most of all. Amen.

The Father Wants to Give You Good Things

What father among you would hand his son a snake when he asks for a fish? Or hand him a scorpion when he asks for an egg? If you then, who are wicked, know how to give good gifts to your children, how much more will the Father in heaven give the holy Spirit to those who ask him? (Luke 11:11–13)

Can you imagine asking your parents for scrambled eggs for breakfast and instead being served a plate of fried scorpions? You'd sure be surprised — and probably a little angry.

But your parents would never do that, would they? Because they know what you need, and they do their best to give it to you. They have your well-being in mind when they make decisions. Sure, sometimes they say no to things you ask for, but when you ask for something that's good for you, they are happy to give it if they can.

That's even more true of God the Father! There is nothing He can't give you. In fact, He wants to give you only good things! He wants to give you himself! That's why He sends God the Holy Spirit to us: to help us know and love God even better.

Conversation Starters

- Can you think of some of the good things that God wants to give you?
- What are some of the good things you want to ask God for?

Prayer

Dear God, thank You for wanting only good things for me. Please help me to remember that You see what I need and are always willing to give it to me. Amen.

The Father's Love Is Sacrificial

For God so loved the world that he gave his only Son, so that everyone who believes in him might not perish but might have eternal life. (John 3:16)

Have you ever had to be away from someone you love? Maybe you miss your dad while you're at school. Maybe your mom sometimes takes business trips. Maybe your grandparents live far away, and you only get to see them once a year.

It's hard to be away from the people you love, isn't it?

When someone we love is far away, we miss them and count down the time until we can be together again.

God the Father and Jesus love each other more than we can even imagine, yet the Father was willing to send Jesus to earth to suffer and die for us, because it was the only way to bring us to heaven someday.

What an incredible sacrifice! What a sign of love from God the Father!

Conversation Starters

- Are there people that you miss when they're gone?
- How does it make you feel to know that God loves you so much?
- Is there any way that you can thank Him?

Prayer

Dear Father, thank You for sending Jesus to me. Please help me to know and understand just how much You love me. Amen.

The Father Loves Us Enough to Discipline Us

For whom the LORD loves he reproves,
as a father, the son he favors. (Proverbs 3:12)

Loving someone isn't the same as being nice. When we're nice, we want everything to be pleasant and agreeable. But when we truly love people, we want them to be the greatest versions of themselves. We want the best for them, and sometimes that means we have to correct them.

None of us is perfect, and there's a good chance that at least once every day we will make a mistake. We will act in a way that is not our best. We will hurt someone else or ourselves. Sometimes we don't even notice we're making a mistake. We need someone to tell us that we have done something wrong — not so we can be punished, but so we can correct our mistakes and do better next time.

This is what God wants to do for us. He wants to point out the times we get it wrong — not so we feel ashamed or embarrassed, but so we can be our greatest selves. He corrects us because He loves us so much.

Conversation Starters

- Can you think of a time when your parents corrected or disciplined you? What happened? What was their purpose? What did you learn from it?

PRAYER

Dear God, thank You for loving me enough to care about the times when I get it wrong.
Thank You for loving me enough to be more than just nice to me. Amen.

God the Father Forms Us Gently

Yet, Lord, you are our father;
we are the clay and you our potter:
we are all the work of your hand. (Isaiah 64:7)

Have you ever seen a potter at work? It takes a long time and a lot of patience to work with clay.

A potter will start his work by placing a lump of wet clay on the center of his wheel. Spinning the wheel, he'll slowly run his hands along the outside of the lump of clay, applying just the right amount of pressure to form the soft clay into the shape he wants. All the while, he'll make sure that the clay stays wet and pliable, making small adjustments here and there. The whole time a potter is creating, his hands are touching the clay. He works slowly, gently, and with great patience.

In the end, the potter creates something beautiful and completely unique. He might be able to make two pieces that look similar, but no two vases or cups or bowls he makes will be exactly the same.

God is like a potter. He works slowly and carefully, molding us and shaping us into something beautiful. No two of us are the same, but if we let God work in our lives, we will be wonderful.

Conversation Starters

- Have you ever watched a potter work? Would you ever like to create something with clay?
- Why do you think God compares Himself to a potter?
- How are we like God's clay?

Prayer

Dear God, thank You for loving me enough to be patient and slow with me. Help me to be patient with myself as You shape me and mold me into someone beautiful. Amen.

The Father Sees What Is Done in Secret

But when you pray, go to your inner room, close the door, and pray to your Father in secret. And your Father who sees in secret will repay you. (Matthew 6:6)

God the Father sees you even when no one else does. He is there for each and every moment of your life. You can be certain that He sees the good you do, even when it feels like no one else does.

If you ever feel lonely or unseen, simply call out His name and tell Him. He will listen and strengthen your heart and make sure that you have all that you need.

Conversation Starters

- Have you ever felt unseen? What was that like?
- How does it make you feel to know that God sees all the good you do?

Prayer

Dear Lord, thank You for always loving me and always seeing me. Please help me to experience Your Presence with me when I am lonely. Amen.

The Father Notices Every Single Thing about You

Are not five sparrows sold for two small coins? Yet not one of them has escaped the notice of God. Even the hairs of your head have all been counted. Do not be afraid. You are worth more than many sparrows. (Luke 12:6–7)

Can you count how many hairs you have? I know I can't. I think I'd lose count just trying to figure out how many hairs are in a single section of my ponytail. If I ever managed to figure it out, I'd probably have to count again as soon as I finished, because hair always seems to fall out, doesn't it?

But God knows. He always knows exactly how many hairs are on your head at any given time. Isn't that mind-boggling? He cares so much about you that He pays attention to even the teeniest, tiniest details about you.

Your favorite color? He knows it, down to the exact shade.

Your favorite line in your favorite television episode? He knows.

He loves to watch you smile, and He loves the sound of your laugh.

Conversation Starters

- What does it tell you about God that He has counted every hair on your head?
- How does it make you feel that God knows you so deeply?
- What do you think is God's favorite part about you?

Prayer

Dear God, sometimes it's hard to remember that You know me down to the tiniest detail. Help me to remember that You are always paying attention to me. Amen.

The Father Made Us to Be Like Him

God created mankind in his image;
in the image of God he created them;
male and female he created them. (Genesis 1:27)

When people see a new baby, one of the very first things they talk about is who the baby looks like. Eager family members line up to examine whether the baby looks like mom or dad. They want to see whether there's any resemblance to siblings or grandparents.

Even if you don't look like anyone else in your family, there is one Person you will see when you look in the mirror: God. You were made in His image and likeness, and that goes much deeper than your hair or eye color.

Being made in God's image means that we can discover something about God from His image within us. When we speak of the "mystery" of God, what we mean is that God is so great that no one can fully grasp His nature or essence. He has, however, revealed himself to us in Jesus, His Son, and by the gift of the Holy Spirit. Because we know in faith that we are made in His image, we revere that image in every man, woman, and child, and in a sense, we can "see God" in others.

Conversation Starters

- Are there parts of yourself where you see God the most clearly?
- Where do you see God in others?

Prayer

Dear God, thank You for making me like You. Please help me to show others who You are by letting them see my true self. Please help me to see You in the people around me. Amen.

God the Father Has a Place for You

Do not let your hearts be troubled. You have faith in God; have faith also in me. In my Father's house there are many dwelling places. If there were not, would I have told you that I am going to prepare a place for you? (John 14:1–2)

Jesus tells us here that God's house has many rooms — and He has one for each of us. God the Father doesn't just jumble us all together, like siblings sharing a bedroom. The place God has for you will be uniquely *yours* — yours and His.

Let's take a moment to imagine: What do you think the place God has prepared for you might look like? What will you see there? What will you feel? What will you hear or smell? How will this place tell you that God loves you deeply?

Conversation Starters

- How do you feel when you hear that God has a place for you?
- What does it tell you about God that He has made a dwelling for you in His house?
- What do you think the place God has picked out for you will look like?

Prayer

Dear Father, thank You for preparing a place for me. Thank You for loving me enough to want me with You always. Amen.

God Is the Father of Lights

All good giving and every perfect gift is from above, coming down from the Father of lights, with whom there is no alteration or shadow caused by change. (James 1:17)

Fireflies. Aurora borealis. Twinkling stars. Phosphorescent algae. Glow-in-the-dark fish. In every dark place, God the Father also put a light. The darkest night, the deepest ocean — these all have creatures and objects that sparkle.

In life, there will be times of darkness. We live in a fallen world, so bad days cannot be avoided. However, just as He does in nature, God will always provide a light for you in your darkest hours. You simply have to know where to look and how to see it.

The easiest way to find the light in your life is to know who God is, because God is the Father of Lights. All lights come from Him, because He is light. If you know God, you will be able to see the lights He has placed in your life.

Conversation Starters

- Do you have a favorite source of light?
- What does it tell us about who God is when Saint James calls Him the Father of Lights?
- Have you ever experienced a hard time? Did you notice any lights God placed in your life?

Prayer

Dear Father of Lights, thank You for all of the lights You have put in my life.
Please help me to always be able to see them clearly. Amen.

God Wants to Be the One You Love the Most

He said to him, "You shall love the Lord, your God, with all your heart, with all your soul, and with all your mind. This is the greatest and the first commandment." (Matthew 22:37–38)

The very first commandment God gave Moses was that His people should not have any other gods. Jesus repeats this commandment in another way: He tells the disciples that they should love God more than anyone or anything else.

Is this because God is selfish? Greedy? Jealous?

No. It's because He knows what we need to be happy. God knows that if we love Him the most, we will listen to Him more than anyone else. He can't ever lead us the wrong way — He can't lie to us, disappoint us, or hurt us — so if we love Him the most, our hearts will be protected and safe.

Conversation Starters

- What does it tell us about God that He wants us to love Him with all of our being?
- Do you love God with all your heart, with all your soul, and with all your mind?
- What can you do to grow in love of God?

Prayer

Dear Father, please help me today and every day to love You more than anyone or anything else in my life. Amen.

The Father Calls You His Child

See what love the Father has bestowed on us that we may be called the children of God. Yet so we are. The reason the world does not know us is that it did not know him. Beloved, we are God's children now; what we shall be has not yet been revealed. We do know that when it is revealed we shall be like him, for we shall see him as he is. (1 John 3:1–2)

God loves you so much that He calls you His child.

You, right now, as you read this book, are one of God's children. Without having to try or work extra hard or win a contest, just by the simple fact of your existence, you are God's child. And that is a fact that can fill you with wonder if you sit and think about it.

The God of the universe, the one who made heaven and earth and every single thing in it, calls you His child. You have always been and always will be His child, no matter what you do or don't do during your life. He loves you. As His child, God the Father makes you a promise in this passage. Can you find it?

Yes! Someday we will get to see God just as He is. We will get to see Him face-to-face. We will get to look at Him and fully understand who He is. Isn't that incredible?

Conversation Starters

- What do you think it means to be God's child? What benefits or responsibilities do you think that comes with?
- What do you think it will be like to see God as He really is? What do you think you'll say to Him when you meet him?

Prayer

Dear Father, thank You for calling me Your child. Thank You for loving me right here and right now, in this very moment. Help me to always feel You with me and to get to know you better each day. Amen.

God's Plans Stand Forever

But the plan of the LORD stands forever,
the designs of his heart through all generations. (Psalm 33:11)

When we have something important to say, we usually say it more than once. For example, when we love someone, we tell them that many times — sometimes many times in a single day. It's so important that we don't want them to forget, and we remind them as often as possible.

This psalm isn't the only place in the Bible where God the Father reminds us that His plans stand forever. He says this a lot. God knows that sometimes we need to be reassured that He will not let us down.

The plans of God's heart stand forever. What does that mean? What are the plans of God's heart? I bet you can guess the biggest, greatest plan of God's heart. It was Jesus.

From the very beginning, when Adam and Eve sinned, God planned to send Jesus to save us, to die for us, and to open heaven back up to us. He did that because He loves us and wants us to be with Him always.

God also knew that it would be thousands of years before Jesus would come, so He spoke words of reassurance and hope for His people while they waited for a Savior. He often reminded them that He wouldn't give up on them, even when they made mistakes or disappointed Him.

Conversation Starters

- How does it make you feel that God's plans stand forever?
- God does not stop loving us, no matter how many mistakes we make. Do you think you could have that much patience?

Prayer

Thank You, God, for keeping Your promises. When I am feeling impatient or disappointed, help me to remember how much You love me. Amen.

God Is on Your Side

What then shall we say to this? If God is for us, who can be against us? He who did not spare his own Son but handed him over for us all, how will he not also give us everything else along with him? (Romans 8:31–32)

God is on your side.

No matter what difficulties you face, no matter what sufferings come your way, God is there with you, working for your good. He wants the best for you and will never give up on you.

You can trust Him.

Conversation Starters

- What types of circumstances can you think of where it would be really good to have God on your side?
- How does it make you feel to have God on your side?

Prayer

Thank You, God, for being on my side. Help me to turn to You when I am in trouble. Help me to rely on You when I am in need. Amen.

God Won't Forget You

Can a mother forget her infant,
be without tenderness for the child of her womb?
Even should she forget,
I will never forget you. (Isaiah 49:15)

Everyone forgets things. Sometimes we forget to bring our lunch to school. Sometimes we forget to take out the trash or do our chores. Sometimes we forget to pack our sneakers for gym class.

But it's hard to imagine a mom forgetting her baby, isn't it?

That's why God uses this image. He's trying to tell you that even if something unimaginable happens, even if the craziest things you can think of really do happen in the world, He still won't forget you.

Think about that for just a moment: You are always on God's mind. He is always thinking about you. You matter that much to Him.

Conversation Starters

- What's the craziest thing that you can imagine happening? Do you believe that even if it did happen, God won't forget you?
- How does it make you feel to know that you are always on God's mind?

Prayer

Dear God, thank You for reminding me that You are a constant in my life. Thank You for promising that You will never forget about me. Please help me to trust You. Amen.

Going Further

I hope that when your family reaches the end of this book, it doesn't mean it will be the end of your journey with the Bible.

In this book, I provided twenty Scripture passages and meditations that you can use as a family, but there are many other passages of the Bible that you can read and pray with together! The daily and Sunday Mass readings are a great place to begin if you're feeling overwhelmed. To help guide your discussions, you can use the following open-ended questions as a starting point for any Scripture discussion:

- What does this passage tell us about God's love?
- What did you notice about God's identity?
- What words stick out to you?
- What is God's promise to us in this passage?
- How does that make you feel?

Notes for Parents

DEUTERONOMY 1:30–31

It can be hard to see God's hand in the journey of our lives. Most of us adults can point to moments in our past when we desperately wished to see God move in a specific way, but He didn't, or times when we felt we could have used His consolation, but it didn't come.

It can be difficult to grasp a verse like this, when perhaps our lived experience contradicts it. I've been there myself.

Sometimes we can look back and see how the pieces of the puzzle fell into place and understand how God was working and moving through painful challenges. But sometimes we can't, and we struggle to trust that He is with us in our suffering. But you don't have to sit in that struggle without hope. There is healing available if you want it. The work of Dr. Bob Schuchts and Neal Lozano are wonderful places to begin.

JEREMIAH 1:5

As parents, we know our children intimately. When my own kids were babies, I held them and gazed at them until I knew the meaning of every single look that crossed their faces. Even as they've grown older, I know them because I pay attention to them. God loves and knows them, too, except in an infinitely deeper sense.

A wonderful way to help children understand this more concretely is to point out some of their tiny traits that you notice. What are some things that a person who just met them might not know, but you do? For example, I know that when my eldest gets anxious, she wrings her hands. I know that my son has three tiny freckles on the side of his face, a feature he shares with his three uncles.

How does it make your children feel that you notice these things about them? How many more details must God notice — details that escape even us parents?

ISAIAH 54:10

This is one of my very favorite passages in the Bible. I have clung to it many times over the years and always find comfort in remembering that God will stand by me, even when my world is falling apart.

The simple yet vivid imagery of the passage makes it relatable to kids, who can get lost in some of the more complicated stories and theology of the Bible. This is a straightforward promise from God the Father to them, with no qualifiers or exceptions. God won't leave, and He won't stop loving us. No *if*s, *and*s, or *but*s.

JEREMIAH 29:11–14

Sometimes sharing our faith journey with our children can feel too daunting (or for some of us, not G-rated). Please don't let that stop you.

This passage offers an open door for talking with your children about the adventure God has taken you on. Are there any significant episodes in your journey that you can share? When did you go looking for God with your whole heart? What happened?

This passage also serves as a reminder that following God is not boring or dull, contrary to the many stereotypes of "church ladies." If you're struggling to share your own story with your kids, consider talking about the many saints that God has taken on adventures. St. Francis Xavier's life is a wonderful example of a literal adventure for the younger crowd. Other saints you might want to share with your children are: St. Teresa of Ávila, St. Catherine of Siena, St. Maximilian Kolbe, Bl. Carlo Acutis, and Sts. Jacinta and Francisco Marto.

ISAIAH 41:13

This can be one of the more difficult passages for us parents to teach our children, because most of us have had enough life experience to know just how scary the world can be. We want to shield our kids from the world's terrors, and to a certain degree, that's the right thing to do. It's our job to allow our children to be children, to spare them as best we can from things that are too much for them to bear. Young children are not ready for all the horrors of the world, but they do need to know that the world we live in is a fallen one, because they need to know who to turn to when they encounter its brokenness.

My husband and I have tried to walk that fine line with our children, and while our approach might not be right for every family, I'd like to share what works for us. We make sure that we explain with compassion any instances of poverty or pain that they see. If we see a man or woman begging on the side of the road, we offer food and a smile, and we always ask for the person's name, so that we can pray for them. We do not sugarcoat the realities of illness and death for our children. We always honestly answer the questions that our children ask, with age-appropriate language, even if they hit a topic that we hadn't planned on broaching yet. We want to build trust with our kids. If they realize that we will be open, honest, and direct with them now, they will be more likely to come to us later in life when they are grappling with bigger issues.

However, as we do this, we also offer them the hope of Christ — the reality that this world we live in is not our final destination. We were created to be with God in heaven for eternity. This is where the lives of the saints are invaluable; they show us that it is possible to maintain peace, joy, and hope, even in the midst of terrible trials.

LUKE 12:22–27

When my kids study ecosystems, I love the way it gives us more opportunities to marvel at God's creation. The more they learn about the world around them, the more they are awed by just how much attention to detail creation requires.

This allows me to point them toward God's greatest creations: themselves. If God paid so much attention to the voltage of electricity in electric eels or the pattern of blinks in a firefly's light, how much more attention would He have given to their creation? How much thought, how much effort, how much attention to detail in planning every part of them!

LUKE 11:11–13

The caveat for this verse is that sometimes we ask God for something that is not good for us. Depending on the age of your children, this is a good verse for talking about the differences between our ways and God's way — and between God's vision and our own. The Father sees all the moving pieces in the world. We, on the other hand, only see our little slice of it.

Rarely do we ask God for something that we know is bad for us, but sometimes we do ask Him for things that we mistakenly think are good — and then God says no. This hurts, especially when we don't understand why God has turned us down.

Underlying this passage is the truth that God wants us to ask Him for things (yes, even us parents— we too are God's children).

Children are dependent on their parents, and they have the right to express their needs. Part of my job as a mom is to teach my children how to go to God with their needs. This means that I model prayer, and I show them that I also ask for what I need from the Lord. I teach them how to speak to God with respect — but also with intimacy and love. I strive to model expectant faith rather than concrete expectations. We can trust that God will move and will respond to our prayers, even though the outcome might be different than the one we want.

JOHN 3:16

This passage from John is possibly the most often-quoted verse from the New Testament. As a result, it's one of the easiest to overlook, to take for granted, to gloss over. But when I pause and sit with this truth — that God sent His Son to die for us, so that we could regain the eternal life we lost through our own sin — I am overcome by the immensity of it, by the passion and strength of His love.

This love calls for a response from my own heart. This is what I like to focus on with my children as we talk about this passage. Depending on their age, I'll share some of the ways that I try to respond to God's love. For younger children, we'll talk about how spending time with God shows Him we love Him, using Mass and Eucharistic adoration as examples. For older children, I'll share about my personal prayer time and the importance of spiritual reading and journaling in my relationship with God.

PROVERBS 3:12

This passage helps me to remember my own goals as a parent. My job is to help my kids get to heaven, to fully become the people that God created them to be. This means that I need to focus on reprimands and discipline, not punishments, and when I shift my perspective that way, my attitude toward their mistakes shifts, too. I am more likely to be patient and calm when I focus on imitating the Father and helping them to learn and grow.

This passage also reminds me that I need to be willing to receive God's corrections in my own life. I may be an adult, but I am very much still growing in my faith. I need God the Father to tell me when I'm not on the right path, and I need to take His reproofs with humility, remembering that they come from Love Himself.

ISAIAH 64:7

Sometimes as adults we can think that God the Father works more like a sculptor than a potter — that He takes His chisel and whacks at our hard surfaces, chipping away at us to create His perfect piece of art. We might even want Him to do that: to solve a problem quickly, to smash away a part of us that we don't like (or a part of someone else that we don't like). The reality, though, is that throughout the Bible, God uses the analogy of a potter to describe His work in us. A potter works slowly, gently, and with great patience. If a potter works too fast or presses too hard, his piece will be ruined. God works with similar patience, always making small adjustments while always, always keeping His hands on us. We need to be patient with ourselves and others as we allow God to work in us.

MATTHEW 6:6

Some of the most powerful moments in my motherhood occur when I notice my child's small act of kindness or sacrifice, and I quietly let them know that I saw. I don't make a big show of it, but I always try to make sure that they feel seen. I want them to know that their quiet actions matter. Showing my kids that I notice the little things they do helps them to believe that God, who sees even more than I do, sees everything, even if their good deeds are overlooked by the people around them.

LUKE 12:6–7

This reading provides a great opportunity to talk to your children about how much God delights in them.

This passage shows us that our value to God is not dependent on what we do or accomplish, but simply on the fact that we are. Our being is enough. We exist because we are valuable to God, valuable enough to warrant His attention — an attention so detailed that He knows the number of hairs on our heads.

That's an intimate love that I'm sure most of us feel like we don't deserve — and we don't!

God's love for us is a pure gift. This is a wonderful lesson for kids, especially when they might be struggling to fit in or having a hard time figuring out what they're good at. We all go through those phases in life, and the more we can help our children understand their value and their worth as God does, the easier it will be for them to navigate these phases.

GENESIS 1:27

Being made in the image and likeness of God is at the very heart of our identity, but sometimes we can take this passage in Genesis for granted, because we have heard it so many times. However, if we stop and think about the dignity of each individual life — that each one of us is made in God's image — it will change how we see ourselves and others.

One of the best ways you can affirm your child is to point out the parts of them that magnify and reflect the Lord's identity. Is your child especially generous? Is she patient? Did he just do something kind? All of these moments, big and small, can be opportunities to remind them that they were made to be like God.

This is a good place to note that as adults, we know that God is neither physical nor limited. We're made in His image, but that truth is much more than our appearance, our personalities, or our gifts. The meditation that goes along with this passage omits many theological concepts. That was deliberate, and I'd like to explain why.

When I begin to teach the concept of numbers to my kids (usually around age two or three), we begin with the number one. We count to five, and we practice the concept of numbers getting larger and smaller in measurable, concrete ways, such as counting rocks or steps or dogs we see on a walk. I keep my lessons simple because I am laying a foundation, and there is a great deal that I leave out. Toddlers aren't ready to understand the concepts of decimals, fractions, negative numbers, or even the concept of zero, so I don't mention them at all. Does this mean I am lying to my children? No. I'm meeting them where they are and giving them the knowledge about numbers that they are able to grasp.

I do the same thing when I teach my children about the Lord. We begin with the concrete and move to the abstract when they are ready. The meditation for this passage uses concrete examples to help highlight the concept of what it means to be "like God." Depending on how old your child is and where they are in their faith journey, they may be ready to move past the metaphor of looking in the mirror and dive deeper into the parts of their identity that are like God.

JOHN 14:1–2

Belonging. Every child wants to belong, to fit in, to have a place, yet so many children experience the pain of not feeling part of a group. We as adults have felt this, too! The truth is that our hearts' desire for acceptance is from God. He is calling us back to Him, and our hearts know that, as Saint Augustine said so eloquently. To paraphrase: We won't rest until we rest in Him.

The earlier we root our children's identity and sense of belonging in God the Father, the easier it will be for them when they inevitably find themselves in a situation in which they are the outsider. As we teach them that each and every one of us has a special place in God's heart, they will be more likely to be inclusive of others.

JAMES 1:17

The idea that our children will experience the darkness of the world can be a scary thought for us parents, but the reality is that we live in a fallen world, and the effects of sin and death are all around us. As much as I'd like to shield my children from this reality, I know that it's much better to prepare them to face it. Therefore, as they get older, we start sharing bits and pieces of our own faith lives with them, as well as the places where God has given us lights in the dark.

Consider sharing with your children about a hard time in your life — a time when things seemed overwhelming, when you didn't see a path forward, or when you felt alone. Talk to them about how you felt, and then explain the way your faith helped you through. Show them how God lit your way, even when you were uncertain, and how He offered you consolation during trials.

MATTHEW 22:37–38

One of the hardest parts about raising kids is knowing that someday they are going to grow up and have their hearts broken. Eventually, someone is going to wound, disappoint, or hurt them. This is an inescapable effect of the fallen world we live in, but if we teach our children how to love God above anyone or anything else, we can help mitigate the hurt. We can't prevent it, but we can ensure that it will not knock them down for long.

1 JOHN 3:1–2

Tradition tells us that the Gospel writer and beloved disciple John wrote this passage. It was John who reclined at Christ's side at the Last Supper, laying his head on Jesus' chest, and it was John who first recognized the Risen Lord at the Sea of Gennesaret. One of the many things I have learned over the years from reading and sitting with John's writings is that getting to know God is like getting to know other people: It takes closeness, intentionality, and time.

If we remain close to the Father, He will change our hearts and slowly conform them to His. Reminding myself that I am His child helps me when I struggle to feel connected to God. Sitting with this passage and letting myself wonder at this great honor is a surefire way for me to regain a grateful heart.

Though not the subject of this meditation, there is another key part of this passage: Sometimes the world does not understand us. This might be a helpful truth to meditate on if your child is struggling to fit in or is feeling misunderstood.

PSALM 33:11

God plays the long game, and we parents need to as well. The faith that we are hoping to cultivate in our children requires a lifetime to develop. As the popular saying goes, it's a marathon, not a sprint. Some days/months/years it may feel like the truth you are pouring into your children about the Catholic Faith is not bearing any fruit. I encourage you not to be disheartened in those moments. As the Lord says in Isaiah 55:11, "*So shall my word / be that goes forth from my mouth; / It shall not return to me empty, / but shall do what pleases me, / achieving the end for which I sent it.*"

ROMANS 8:31–32

When Saint Paul wrote this letter to the Romans, he was offering them encouragement and hope. The "everything else" that he spoke of wasn't meant in the worldly sense; rather, he was reassuring them that God the Father, who had given up His own

Son for them, would absolutely, without fail, pour out the Holy Spirit upon them and provide all of the spiritual gifts and graces they would need. This context is important when speaking about this passage with kids who are more legalistic or literal in their interpretations.

ISAIAH 49:15

We adults know that all too often in this broken world, parents do fail to love their children well. For me, this passage is a reminder that even when I fail as a mom, the Father remains perfect. He loves my children with perfect love, and He will not fail or forget them. Even in the midst of sin and suffering and pain that we often cannot understand, God remains. He doesn't promise to take away all of our problems, but He does promise to be present to us in the midst of them. It's a reminder I need to hear often.

If your children have already discovered that some moms and dads do not love their children well, don't feel like you have to shy away from this passage. It can offer the opportunity for them to talk about the hurts they carry or the questions they have.

About the Author

Colleen Pressprich is a former missionary and former Montessori teacher turned homeschooling mom who strives to use the lessons she learned in the mission field and the classroom to live her dream of growing the domestic church. She is the author of *Marian Consecration for Families with Young Children*, *The Women Doctors of the Church*, and *The Jesse Tree for Families*. She lives with her husband, children, and mom in Michigan, where she loves everything about spring, summer, and fall and absolutely hates the winter.

About the Illustrator

Amy Heyse is a Catholic artist who lives in Fort Collins, Colorado, with her husband, two daughters, and cat. Her favorite way to connect to God is through creating, and she loves to make artwork inspired by her prayer life. She has worked as a painting instructor for the past ten years and enjoys teaching artists of all ages. When she's not working on art, she loves watching movies and reading while snuggled up in her favorite bathrobe. You can learn more about her work at amyheyse.com.